P9-DVT-344

Amazing Picture Puzzles

Mazes, Mindbenders, and More

Rolf Heimann

Sterling Publishing Co., Inc.
New York

Library of Congress Cataloging-in-Publication Data available

10 9 8 7 6 5 4 3 2 1

Published by Sterling Publishing Co., Inc.
387 Park Avenue South, New York, NY 10016
This book has been excerpted from Rolf Heimann's Head Spinners
© 1999 by Rolf Heimann; Rolf Heimann's Creepy Conundrums
© 2003 by Rolf Heimann, and Rolf Heimann's Mind Munchers
© 1998 by Rolf Heimann, first published in Australia by Roland Harvey Books.
Distributed in Canada by Sterling Publishing
C/o Canadian Manda Group, One Atlantic Avenue, Suite 105
Toronto, Ontario, Canada M6K 3E7

Printed in China
All rights reserved

Sterling ISBN 1-4027-1322-3

Contents

1. Tentacle Spectacle — 5
2. Mazeville — 6, 7
3. Pyramid — 8
4. Make the Connection — 8
5. Snakesssss! — 9
6. Say Cheese — 10
7. In-Bit-Tweens — 11
8. Snap! — 12, 13
9. Restore the Story — 14
10. Which Zoo — 15
11. Relativity — 16, 17
12. Be a Detective — 18
13. Proverb — 18
14. The Big-Eared Spotted Confuscus — 19
15. Upside-Down Pyramid — 20, 21
16. Movie Disaster — 22, 23
17. Battled by Snakes — 24
18. Garden Gremlins — 25
19. An Eye for an Eye — 26, 27
20. Murder in the Castle — 28, 29
21. Invasion of the Spiny Ant Murderer — 30, 31
22. Beware of the Rogue Robot — 32, 33
23. Skullduggery — 34
24. Critter in a Casket — 34
25. Cockroach Delight — 35
26. Name Bones — 35
27. Dragon Delusion — 36
28. Dragon Drive — 37
29. Haunted Houses — 38, 39
30. Sock It to Me! — 40
31. Dice of Death — 40

32. Gruesome Greenbacks — 41

33. Hiding from Horror — 41

34. Let Sleeping Snakes Lie — 42, 43

35. Blowfly Blitz — 44, 45

36. Beware the Letter Imps — 46, 47

37. The Fuse Has Been Lit — 48, 49

38. Ghostly Words — 50

39. Snake's Tail — 51

40. Baffling Balls — 52

41. Letter Litter — 53

42. Anna Gram Enterprise — 53

43. Treacherous Temple — 54, 55

44. Say What? — 56

45. Fragments from the Pharaohs — 57

46. Forbidden Colors — 57

47. Famous Pairs — 58, 59

48. Pick the Pair — 60

49. Four-Star Puzzle — 61

50. Age by Age — 61

51. Dragon Maze — 62, 63

52. Step by Step — 64

53. Magic Word — 64

54. What Beast Is That? — 65

55. Disk Dilemma — 65

56. Pegs Galore — 66

57. Slot in the Slabs — 67

58. Hexed Paths — 68, 69

59. Find the City — 70

60. Rhyme and Reason — 71

61. Space Captain — 71

62. Mug Shots — 72

63. Math Mystery — 72

64. Star Attraction — 73

Answers — 74

Index — 80

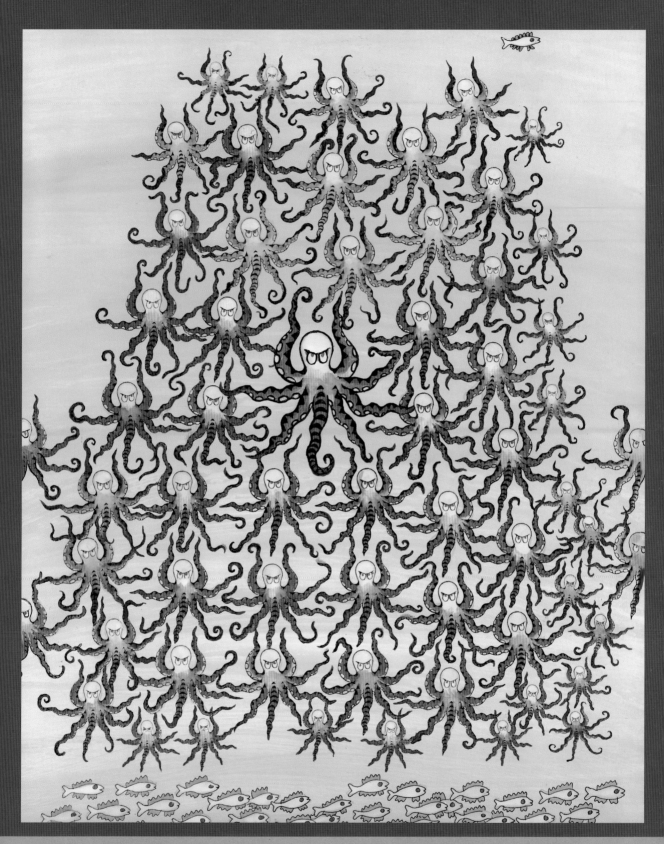

1. Tentacle Spectacle
Rover the yellow sardine has lost his way.
Can he find his way back to his school through the maze of tentacles?
Solution on page 74.

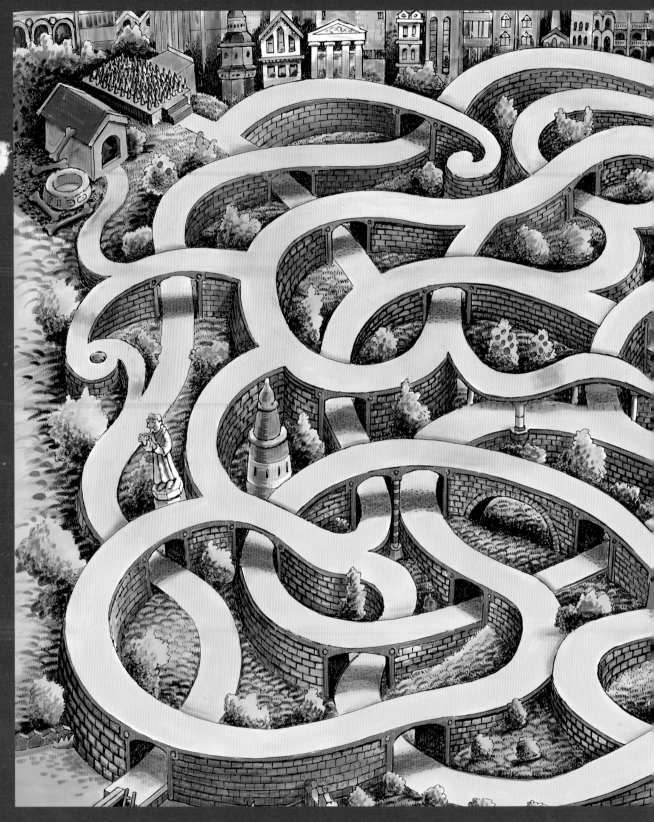

2. Mazeville

Five characters are on their way home to Mazeville.
Can you guess where they live and help them find their way?

Solution on page 74.

That's how the pyramide looks from above:

3. Pyramid

Imagine the pyramid being unfolded, the base being the black triangle. There are several ways of 'unfolding' it, but the arrow must always point to the top and the colors must stay in the same order. Some of the examples are wrong. Which ones?

Solution on page 74.

4. Make the Connection

Find the objects which belong to the people and things below and fill in the corresponding letters. But look carefully, the panels overlap!

Solution on page 74.

5. Snakessssss!

Snakekeeper Enrico has to take Annabelle the Patagonian Asp for her yearly check-up.
So that he could find her, he brought along Annabelle's picture. But spotting her is not so easy, is it?
Before you count them, guess how many snakes there are in this picture: 27? 41? 53?
Solution on page 74.

6. Say Cheese
Five mice are trying to get to the cheese. Will they be able to?
Solution on page 74.

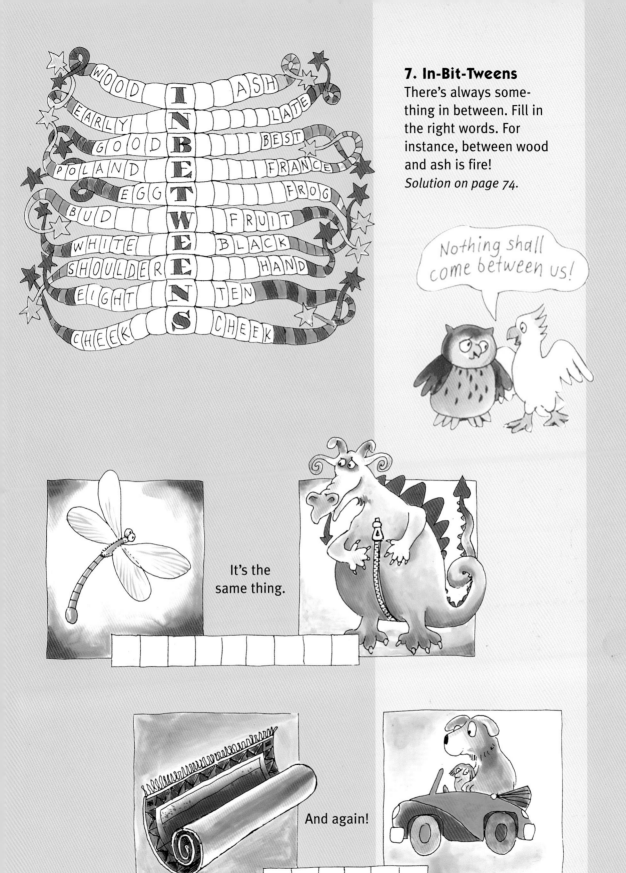

WOOD **IN** ASH
EARLY **B** LATE
GOOD **E** BEST
POLAND **T** FRANCE
EGG **W** FROG
BUD **E** FRUIT
WHITE **E** BLACK
SHOULDER **N** HAND
EIGHT **S** TEN
CHEEK CHEEK

7. In-Bit-Tweens

There's always some-thing in between. Fill in the right words. For instance, between wood and ash is fire!

Solution on page 74.

Nothing shall come between us!

It's the same thing.

And again!

11

8. Snap!

Major McKlink has to make an emergency landing on the planet of Snappio II, which is inhabited by the multicolored Snapponoids. Luckily they are not as dangerous as they look; the only poisonous ones are the two-colored ones. Those with more than two colors are quite harmless. Is there a two-colored Snapponoid among them?

Solution on page 74.

9. Restore the story

Before a film or television commercial is shot, it is customary to draw storyboards, which help to plan camera angles, lighting, props, etc. Sometimes these drawings are done on loose cards which can be moved around. The storyboard cards below have become mixed up, so that the story-line has been lost altogether. Can you put them into the right order? If you are successful, the letters will spell out the name of the film.

Solution on page 74.

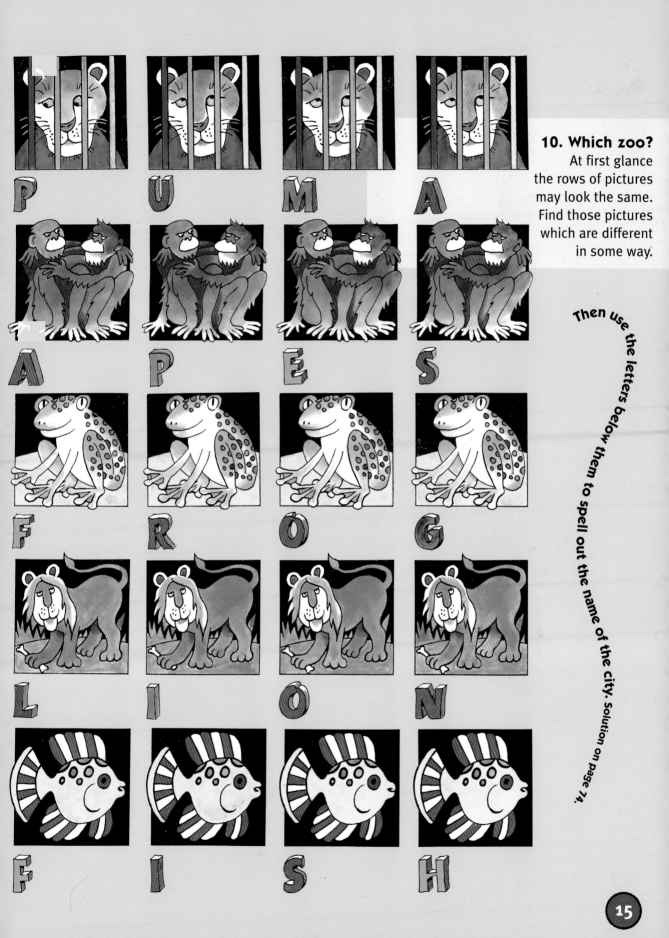

10. Which zoo?

At first glance the rows of pictures may look the same. Find those pictures which are different in some way.

Then use the letters below them to spell out the name of the city. Solution on page 74.

P U M A

A P E S

F R O G

L I O N

F I S H

11. Relativity

Everything is relative! The first answer is given to show you what you are expected to do. Don't just fill in the right words, draw the right thing.

Solution on page 74.

Bicycle is to motorbike as rowboat is to motorboat

Scales are to fish as feathers are to ....

Shoes are to feet as hats are to ....

'E' is to elephant as 'D' is to ....

Road is to car as rail is to ....

New Zealand is to kiwi as Africa is to ....

Window is to house as eye is to ....

'A' is to 'B' as '1' is to ....

Now try making up some on your own! There are some ideas on page 74.

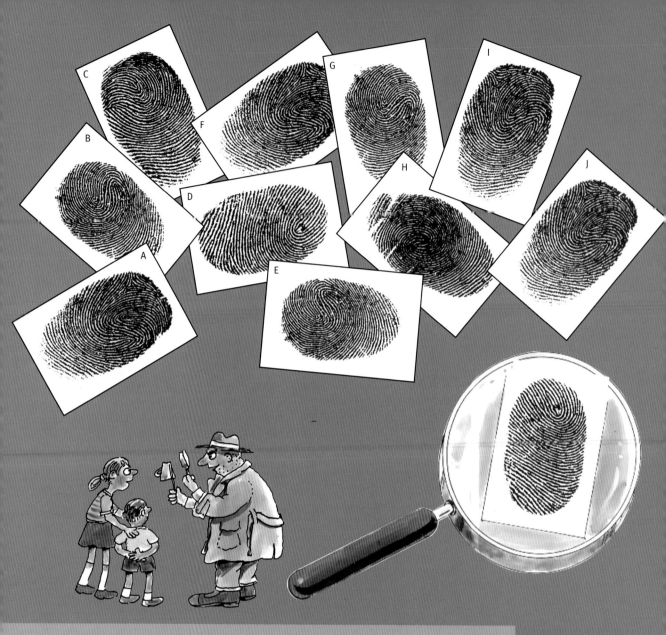

12. Be a Detective!

Fingerprints are a great means of identification.
One of the ten prints is the same as the one under the magnifying glass.
Which one? Be careful, somebody's life might depend on it!
Solution on page 75.

13. Proverb

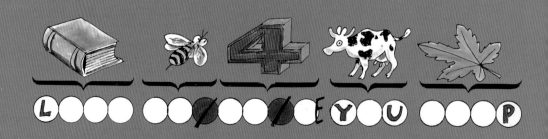

What's the opposite of the big-eared spotted confuscus?

The earless spotless smarticus—which could be me!

14. The Big-Eared Spotted Confuscus

Transfer the lines onto the right squares below. The position of the colored border should be enough of a guide.

Solution on page 75.

15. Upside-Down Pyramid

This upside-down pyramid was built by a tribe of Egyptians who hated its government and therefore did everything the wrong way around. It did not worship cats but hated them. The sign near the entrance, for instance, says; 'Cats go home'. Can you spot the sign inside the tomb, also in hieroglyphics, that says; 'Beware of fools who worship mice'?

You enter the tomb, (which, by the way, they called a 'dimaryp') at one hole and you come out the other, having visited each chamber once only. If you think it can't be done, check on page 75! By the way, did you notice the boy with boots on his hands and gloves on his feet? This is only one of a dozen things these people do the wrong way around. Can you spot the others? And why do you think they called the tomb a 'dimaryp'?

PICNIC ON
HANGING ROC

DATE	SCENE	TAKE
4/6	28	4

16. Movie Disaster

A fire broke out during the filming of 'Xeno the Warrior Grandpa'. No lives were lost, but all the scenery and the costumes were destroyed. It took two weeks to rebuild everything. But nothing ever goes smoothly in the film industry! Director Spiegelbaum discovered lots of mistakes which had to be rectified before filming could continue. What were they?

Solution on page 75.

17. Battled by Snakes

Nothing scares the mighty Scorpion except green rattlesnakes.
Is the Scorpion about to be attacked?
Solution on page 75.

18. Garden Gremlins

Mrs. McGore wants to buy nine new garden gremlins, and she wants all nine to be different. She has already selected five, but can she find four others that are different?

Solution on page 75.

19. An Eye for an Eye
Find your way from one
eye to the other!
Solution on page 76.

20. Murder in the Castle
The old Count of Stankenfrein has been killed.
There is no shortage of murder weapons in the
room, but the police are baffled.

Eight items of evidence, including the murder weapon, have been removed from the scene of the crime. Can you spot them?
Solution on page 76.

21. Invasion of the Spiny Ant Murderer

This spiny ant murderer wants to destroy all ants. The blue ants will be safe if they can find a blue path through the maze.

The white ants will be safe if they can get across to the other side, stepping only on the white lines of the maze. Will both groups of ants escape the spiny ant murderer?
Solution on page 76.

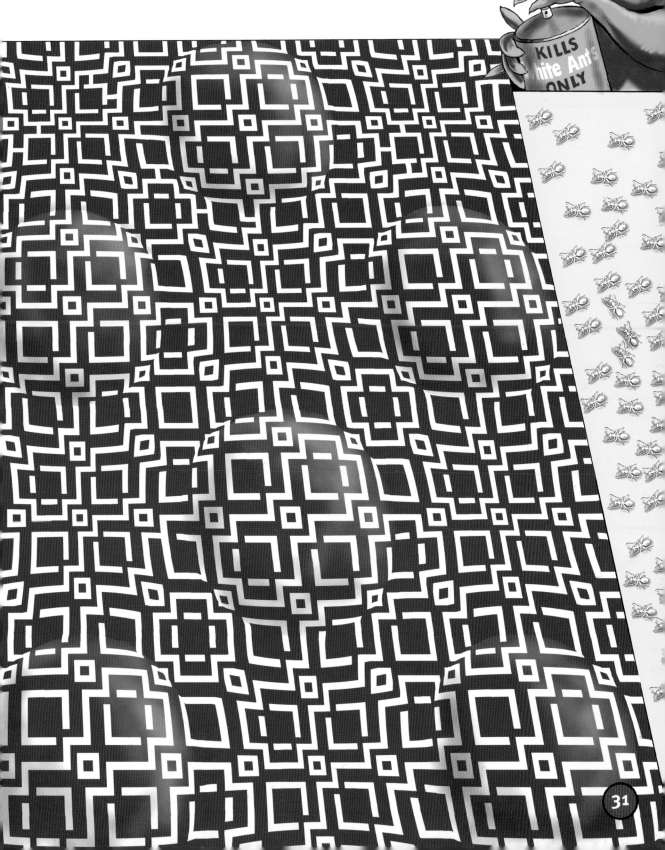

The labels on the robots read: KORKER1, ZIRKULA KEE, SNO VITE, MERAH PUTIH, ZLEEPY, ZEEL, ZAPPA LEONE, ZWIEBELL, ZENN, BARREL O'PHUN, WEBER SHOCK, Y2K, TITANA, ZPIDER, YORKA, HOKO, ZNEERO, RAMBLER, ZOOLY, ZMILER, ZLOE POKE

22. Beware of the Rogue Robot!

One of these robots has mistakenly been programmed to bite people's noses off when they're asleep. Which one is it? Find it quickly so that it can be reprogrammed! (Hint: It has a round head, big pink eyes, and a name that starts with 'Z'.)

Solution on page 76.

23. Skullduggery

Find your way from one arrow
to the other.
There are several ways!
Solution on page 76.

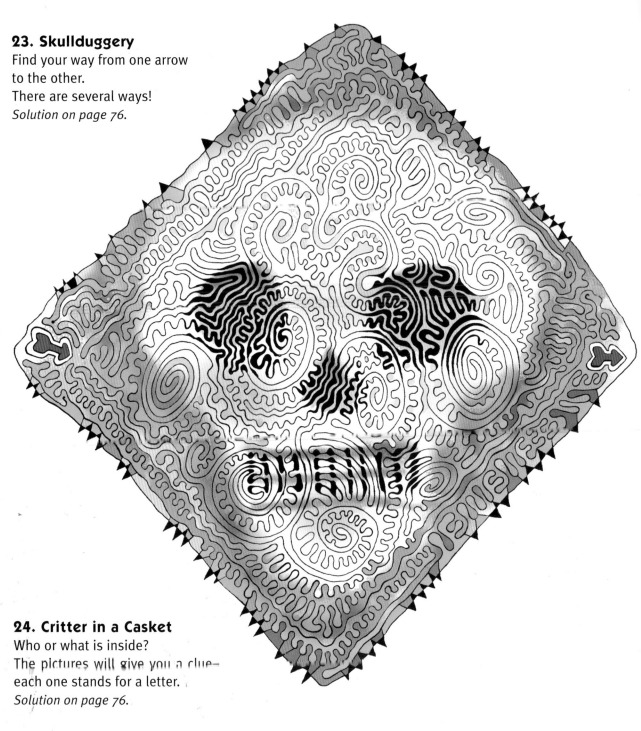

24. Critter in a Casket

Who or what is inside?
The pictures will give you a clue—
each one stands for a letter.
Solution on page 76.

25. Cockroach Delight
'Cockroaches are my favourite food.
Where is my dinner?'
Find the twelve hidden cockroaches.
Solution on page 76.

26. Name Bones
What are the names of the two imps?
They're spelled out with some of the
bones in this picture.
Solution on page 76.

27. Dragon Delusion

Ten of these dragons are identical brothers, but one of them is not. Can you find him?

Solution on page 76.

28. Dragon Drive
The dragon above is closest to you,
but which one is the furthest away
(that is, behind all the others)?
Solution on page 76.

29. Haunted Houses

Can you spot the nine
haunted houses? Here
are five of them.

Other parts of the
city are haunted, too.
Can you find these things?
Solution on page 77.

30. Sock It to Me

Soccerino vampires are not known for their fashion sense, but they do like their socks to match. Socks that do not match are always given to the Needy Monsters. How many socks will have to be thrown away?

Solution on page 77.

31. Dice of Death

These three dice are identical. How many skulls can be seen by Big Eye and its pet spider?

Solution on page 77.

32. Gruesome Greenbacks

The poison of these greenback spiders is always fatal, but if their country of origin is identified, the correct antidote can be given. Which countries do they come from?

Solution on page 77.

33. Hiding from Horror

If you want to know a good place to hide from monsters, unravel this secret message.

Solution on page 77.

34. Let Sleeping Snakes Lie

You need another can of paint to finish painting the wall. Crusher the carpet snake is usually well mannered, but you never know. Can you reach the paint without disturbing her?

Solution on page 77.

35. Blowfly Blitz

Professor Zweistein is breeding a race of supersmart blowflies. Any fly that cannot find its way out of the maze will perish. Is there a way out of the maze?

Solution on page 77.

URANUS FLYTRAP
TYRANOTRAPUS REX

A crow becomes a cow

A comb without an 'M' is a cob

Without an 'O', a boat is a bat

A keel becomes an eel

36. Beware the Letter Imps

By stealing just one letter from each of the things in this picture, the imps turn the objects into something new in the second picture. Can you find all 26 transformations?

Solution on page 77.

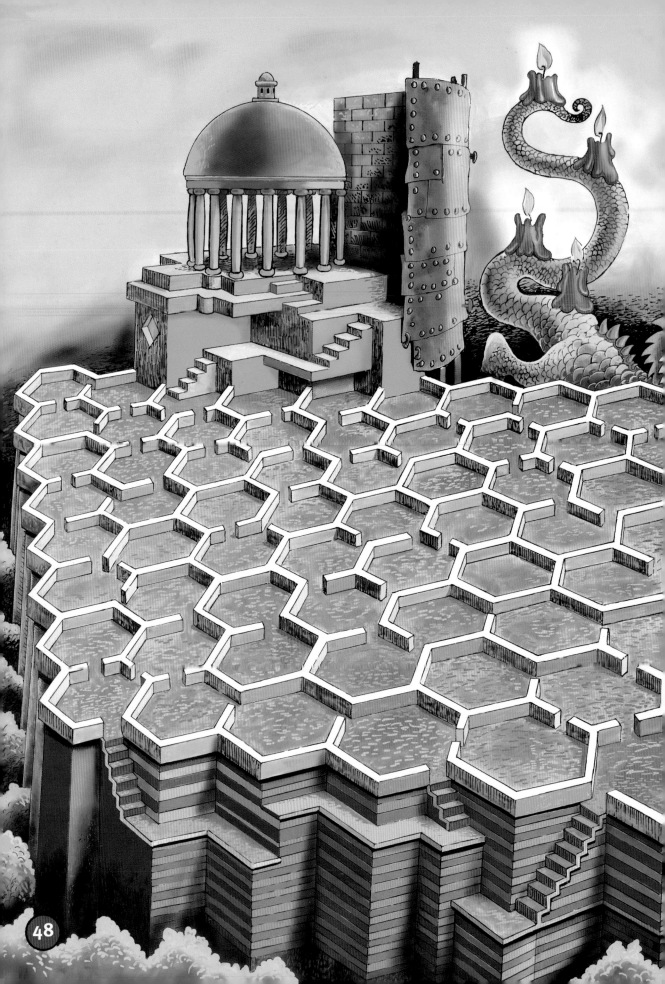

37. The Fuse Has Been Lit

You have only two minutes to find your way from the red building to the safety of the green temple. Go!

Solution on page 77.

38. Ghostly Words

Ten words are hidden in this puzzle. Can you find them all? They may run in any direction, even upwards or diagonally, but always in a straight line.

Solution on page 77.

These are seven of my favorite words

39. Snake's Tail
Which snake's tail will be
chopped off if it's not careful?
Solution on page 77.

40. Baffling balls

At first sight Chico the juggler's balls may all look the same, but two are different.

Two of the balls belong to Chico's friends. Solution on page 78.

52

41. Letter litter

Put these letters in the right order. Make sure the pieces fit snugly!

Solution on page 78.

Go on! What are you afraid of?

42. Anna Gram Enterprises

There is no admittance to the premises of Anna Gram Enterprises. "But why?" wondered Carl. "I think we can find out," said Professor X. "Look, somebody has given us a hint by numbering the letters!"

Solution on page 78.

43. Treacherous temple
This is the temple where once upon a time the faithful sought guidance from Saint Camouflage, the patron saint of people who have things to hide. Fourteen eggs are hidden in the grounds, and those who find them, as well as making their way from the red to the blue flag, are all given praise.

Solution on page 78.

44. Say what?

These three spinster aunts all have their favourite sayings. One day their nephew won the lottery and decided to build a park to honor his aunties by spelling out their words of wisdom. Aunt Claire follows the red ribbon, Aunt Sheila the green, and Aunt Betty goes a step down after each letter.

What are the aunties' favourite sayings? Solution on page 78.

45. Fragments from the Pharaohs

Archaeologists have long been searching for the fragments of a certain ancient Egyptian work of art. Did they find the right ones this time? A total of nine pieces belong in the picture above, but five don't.

Solution on page 78.

46. Forbidden colors

King Nebuchadnezzar's sculptors managed to produce four identical wise men, but one of the painters made a mistake when it came to coloring them. Which of the figures is different and how many mistakes were made?

Solution on page 78.

47. Famous pairs

The names, descriptions and pictures of these famous pairs have been mixed up. Find the right ones, by following the strings if necessary. Just to confuse you, one of them has been made up and doesn't even exist!

LAUREL & HARDY

...were legendary twins who were thrown into the River Tiber. They were rescued by a shewolf, who suckled them. One twin later founded the city of Rome.

Adam & Eve

According to legend, these twins met with disaster after they went up the hill to fetch a pail of water.

GOG & MAGOG

..were created by Mark Twain. The book about two boys' adventures on the Mississippi River became a favorite for children all over the world.

Michael & John Burrington

...were two Americans who began by running a bicycle shop in America. They became the first to achieve motorized flight.

Clark Kent & Lois Lane

Kittyhawk

...were the first twins to fly into outer space, orbiting planet Earth sixty-two times before splashing down into Merri Creek.

ROMEO & JULIET

...were two American bank robbers. They were made famous by a film of the same name, starring Warren Beatty and Faye Dunaway.

Batman & Robin

...were two legendary giants who were captured by the Trojans and made to serve as guardians of a palace in London. In 1708 their statues were erected at the Guildhall in London.

the WRIGHT BROS.

...started as comedy characters in American silent movies, getting into one fine mess after another. One was fat, the other skinny.

Their permanent enemy is "The Joker". But he has no hope of outsmarting these famous fighters for righteousness. They were created in 1939 by Bob Kane as an answer to "Superman".

Tom Sawyer & Huckleberry Finn

Jack & Jill

...were brother and sister in a fairy-tale. Lost in the woods, they were lured into a gingerbread house by a witch. But the children outsmarted her!

BONNIE & CLYDE

Christians believe that these were the first humans created by God. After eating forbidden fruit they were chased from paradise.

Hänsel & Gretel

...were created by William Shakespeare. Despite a feud between their parents, they fell in love, and committed suicide rather than stay apart.

ROMULUS & REMUS

One of them was famous as a fighter for truth, justice, freedom and the American way, and the other followed his exploits for the newspaper, The Daily Planet.

48. Pick the pair
Look for the objects needed by the figures below, then find the attached letters and put them into the corresponding spaces. For example, the monkey's pair is the banana, which is attached to the letter 'T'.
Solution on page 78.

49. Four-star puzzle

Can you trace along the white section of the stars in a single line without lifting your pen from the paper? It can be done, you know!

Solution on page 78.

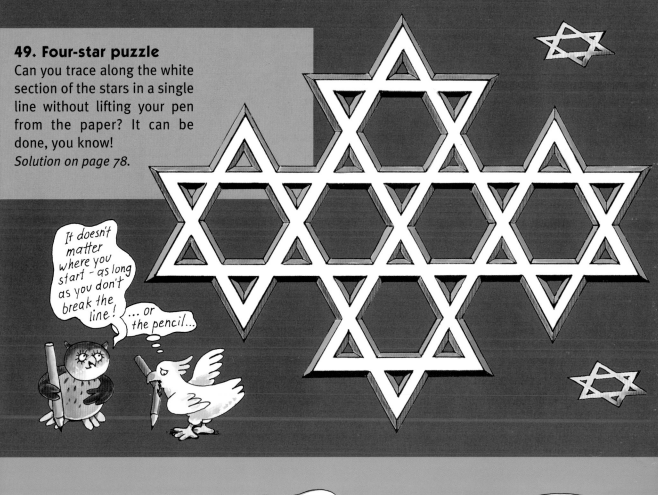

50. Age by age

How old are these children?
You can work it out by studying their clues.

Solution on page 79.

DORA	
BECKA	
TIM	
ROVER	
RUBY	
KARL	
TINA	

51. Dragon Maze

All seven snails will try to make their way through the maze to the leaves on the other side. Not all of them can! Which ones will make it and which ones will not?

Solution: page 79.

52. Step by step

Step from A to Z through the entire alphabet. Start on A, then move to the bell, then to the cloud.

You have to find the rest of the way by yourself. Solution on page 79.

53. Magic word

Find a magic word by collecting all the letters that bear the secret stamp.
Solution on page 79.

This is the secret stamp.

54. What beast is that?

The legendary multiocantor is made up of no less than twelve other animals. Find them all and put their names horizontally into the empty fields.

Solution on page 79.

I think it's a horse!

55. Disk dilemma

When these nine discs are arranged in the right order, the completed stack will display an image. They are keyed to be stacked in one way only. Start from the top or bottom.

Solution on page 79.

No, it must be a snail!

56. Pegs galore

Square pegs don't fit into round holes! The top and bottom rows have already been clicked together. You'll have to work out yourself how the other pieces fit together. Transfer the lines onto the squares of the grid.

Solution on page 79.

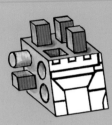

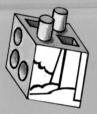

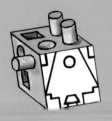

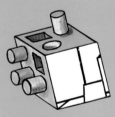

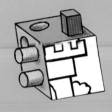

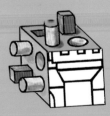

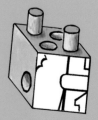

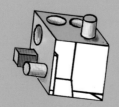

You must pay attention to the shapes...

57. Slot in the slabs

Only one of the blue-sided slabs below fits correctly onto one of the red-sided ones above to make up the design pictured left.
Solution on page 79.

... and the colors as well!

58. Hexed paths
There are eleven ways to make your way through these hexagons, from left to right. Step only through those hexagons whose pictures have something in common.

Starting from the top one, for instance, go only through hexagons with a red background. The second? Use only pictures of pigs. The third path: only fish, the fourth: only animals that look backwards. Then? Try to find other ways!

Solution on page 79.

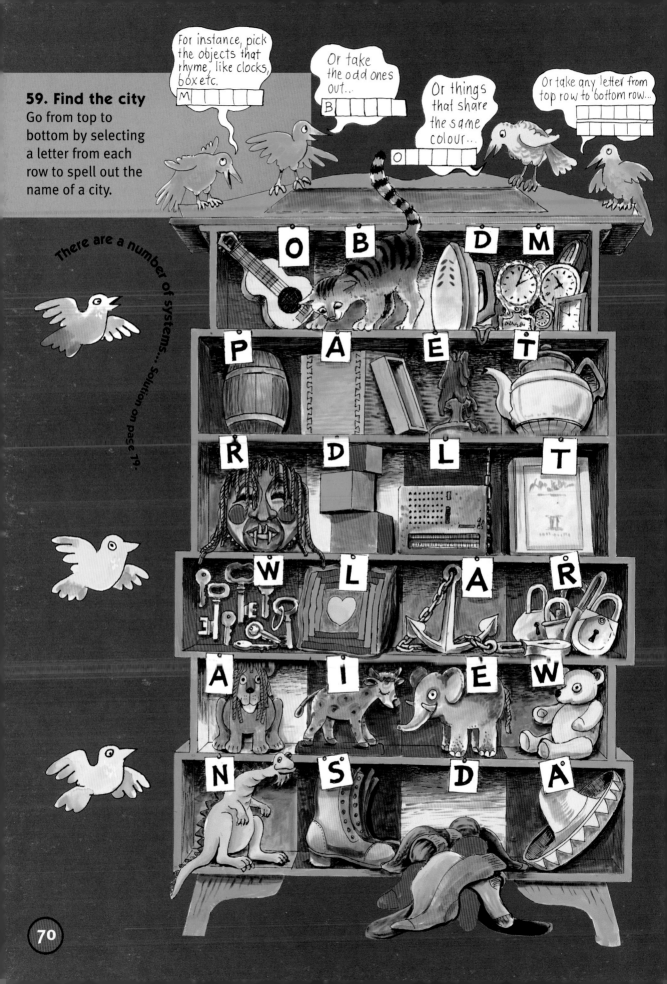

59. Find the city
Go from top to bottom by selecting a letter from each row to spell out the name of a city.

There are a number of systems... Solution on page 79.

60. Rhyme and Reason

Rat rhymes with hat! But that's all the advice you'll get for this puzzle. The other rhymes you'll have to find yourself. If you fill in the right letters, you'll get the name of a famous city.

Solution on page 79.

61. Space Captain

Test your memory—or that of your friends! You are the captain of space patrol No.55 and you are exactly halfway to the galaxy of Nymropia when suddenly another ship appears. A strange green creature from the local Star Watch gets out. According to Intergalactic law you must answer him truthfully. Which question? Before you turn to the next page to read the question, study the picture and this text carefully. If you do, you'll be able to answer.

62. Mug shots

The police are looking for a mystery woman who has been involved in industrial espionage. Luckily they already know a number of things about her.

She has blue eyes, she wears earrings, she has red hair... It shouldn't be too hard to identify her!
Solution on page 79.

63. Math mystery

Elisa made a mistake on the first day of her new job! She had to write down numbers given to her on the phone, but when it came to adding them up, she didn't know whether the paper was the right way up. However, her boss looked at it for a minute and said, "Don't worry, just add it up and be done with it!" Why did he say such a thing?
Solution on page 79.

918
816
886
988